FUN Sports FOR FITNESS

HIKING

Written by

Julie K. Lundgren

Rourke
Educational Media

rourkeeducationalmedia.com

Scan for Related Titles
and Teacher Resources

www.rourkeeducationalmedia.com

PHOTO CREDITS: Cover © Martinmark; Title Page © Efired; Page 4 © Rickshu; Page 5 © SW productions; Page 6 © Alex Raths; Page 7 © Keetten Predators; Page 8 © Maksym Gorpenyuk; Page 9 © Don Bendickson; Page 10 © morganl; Page 11 © Jim Parkin; Page 12 © Jerry Whaley; Page 13 © K McNamara; Page 14 © Steve Lundgren; Page 15 © Robert Dant; Page 16 © Steve Cukrov; Page 17 © Carole Shelley; Page 18 © Anatoily Samara; Page 19 © norcon; Page 20 © William Walsh, Martinmark; Page 21 © Sergiy Zavgorodny; Page 22 © Kapu

Editor: Jill Sherman

Cover Designer: Tara Raymo

Interior Designer:Jen Thomas

Library of Congress PCN Data

Hiking / Julie K.Lundgren
Fun Sports for Fitness
  ISBN 978-1-62169-862-3 (hardcover)
  ISBN 978-1-62169-757-2 (softcover)
  ISBN 978-1-62169-964-4 (e-Book)
Library of Congress Control Number: 2013936467

Also Available as:

ROURKE'S
e-Books

Rourke Educational Media
Printed in the United States of America,
North Mankato, Minnesota

Rourke
Educational Media

rourkeeducationalmedia.com

customerservice@rourkeeducationalmedia.com • PO Box 643328 Vero Beach, Florida 32964

TABLE OF CONTENTS

LET'S GET MOVING

Ready for an adventure on two feet? Hiking offers an easy way for people of all ages and abilities to get outside and get moving. A long walk through the country or woods rewards hikers with awesome views, wildlife, and fresh air.

Simple walks that last a day or less can still lead hikers through amazing natural areas.

People have always hiked, though early people hiked out of need, not for fun. They hunted and gathered food to survive, and used shortcuts and trails to get from one place to another. Today, people hike for health and enjoyment.

HIKING EQUIPMENT

While overnight trips require carrying heavy packs full of camping gear and food, day hikers can pack much less. Get started with a pair of lightweight, sturdy shoes with ankle support and good **traction**. Because new shoes can cause painful blisters, wear them around town or the house for awhile before taking them on the trail. The right socks make a difference, too. Feet in motion get hot and sweaty. Wear socks that take moisture away from the skin, like those made of wool or **synthetics**. Bring an extra pair to change into later.

TRIP TIP

Wear sturdy hiking boots that have excellent traction. Always wear socks to wick away sweat and prevent blisters.

TRIP TIP

Keep blue jeans at home. When wet, jeans lose their ability to keep you warm and take a long time to dry. Instead, choose clothing made from synthetics or wool. This hiker also wears gaiters, an extra layer that protects his lower legs.

Wear a hat to keep sun and rain off your face. Long pants protect legs from biting insects, sunburn, and falls. Wear a watch to keep track of how long you have been on the trail. Pack water, food, a map, **compass**, insect repellent, sunscreen, a warm sweater, first aid kit, and a raincoat in a small backpack. Leave room in your pack for some fun extras like a camera, notebook, or guidebook about animals or plants you may see.

TRIP TIP

Maps and compasses work together to help travelers find their way. Compasses help you find your location on the map by showing you which direction is north. Practice your map and compass skills before your trip.

MAPPING YOUR TRAIL

With a little knowledge and planning, great hikes await. Check out maps of nearby trails in parks, nature areas, and **public lands**. Choose a hike that fits your group's abilities and time. Get a weather report before leaving home. Let someone who is staying home know where you are going and when you plan to return. If you're late, they'll know where to look.

TRIP TIP

Make sure to bring a compass and a good quality topographical map, with specific directions for your hike.

TRIP TIP

If someone is hurt, at least one person should always remain with the injured person. Others in the group should carefully note the location and contact the local forest ranger.

The Appalachian National Scenic Trail passes through Great Smoky Mountains National Park and offers access to other park trails.

NEW HAMPSHIRE
VERMONT
MAINE
PENNSYLVANIA
MASSACHUSETTS
NEW YORK
RHODE ISLAND
CONNECTICUT
OHIO
NEW JERSEY
DELAWARE
W.V.
MARYLAND
KENTUCKY
VIRGINIA
NORTH CAROLINA
TENNESSEE
SOUTH CAROLINA
GEORGIA
FLORIDA
ALABAMA

N
W   E
S

Appalachian National Scenic Trail

Florida National Scenic Trail

The United States has several famous trails over 1,000 miles (1,600 kilometers) long. The Appalachian National Scenic Trail winds 2,175 miles (3,500 kilometers) through fourteen eastern states, with the south end in Georgia and the north end in Maine. Nature lovers can enjoy hikes all year on the Florida National Scenic Trail, a footpath 1,400 miles (2,250 kilometers) long.

TRIP TIP

Hiking is perhaps one of the best ways to enjoy the beauty of nature. It takes most people five to seven months to hike along the Appalachian Trail.

To
Tioga
Road
3.1 mi

2.9 mi (4.7 km)

3 mi (2.1 km)

Yo
Po
693
2114

2.5 mi (4.0 km)

Royal
Arch
Cascade

Royal
Arches

Nort
Pine

Lower
Pines

Middle
Brother

Lower
Brother

inel
alls

7214ft
2199m

Sentinel
Dome
8122ft
2476m

Washburn
Point

.5 mi (2.4 km)

Illilouette Ridge

Sentinel
Dome

Some hikers challenge themselves to hike a very long trail from one end to the other. These thru-hikers may do it all in one trip lasting several months, or hike a few parts of the trail each year until they have hiked the whole thing. Thru-hikes take lots of planning and time, but finishers are rewarded with a great sense of accomplishment and the adventure of a lifetime.

TRIP TIP

What if you have to go to the bathroom and the toilet is miles away? Carefully leave the trail and dig a small hole at least 6 inches (15 centimeters) deep for your deposit. Afterward, refill the hole with dirt. Burying your business keeps it away from animals and other hikers.

TRIP TIP

Geocaching, a new outdoor sport, is like a treasure hunt. Hikers follow clues, a map, and a compass or **GPS** to find a hidden container. Finders can sometimes trade out part of the treasure with small toys, stickers, or other cool things.

TRIP TIP

A walking stick or hiking pole helps hikers keep their balance and offers support.

Trails in nature centers, local parks, and state parks often show off the special natural features in the area. Start at a **trailhead**. Trailheads often have a parking lot, restroom, maps, and trail information. Large trail systems have many trailheads.

SAFETY FIRST

Smart hikers never go alone. They stay on the trail to avoid getting lost. They also prevent falls and twisted ankles by stepping carefully when they see wet rocks, tree roots, mud, and loose gravel.

Carry a whistle in case you get lost. Three blasts signal others that you need help. Wearing bright colors helps searchers find you, too.

Bringing a cell phone might seem like a good idea. But if your hike is close to towns and people, you will most likely not need an emergency phone. Also, using a cell phone on a hike can bother other people who want to listen to nature. On the other hand, if you are in a very remote area, your cell phone will probably not get a signal. It is not a good idea to waste space in your pack with a cell phone.

Insect repellent keeps bugs away. Tuck pants into socks to protect against **ticks**. Check for them during and after the hike, especially along your hairline and on your neck.

Learn how and when to use the items in the first aid kit. Commonly used items include tweezers for tick removal, calomine lotion for rashes and bug bites, and bandages and antibiotic cream for cuts and scrapes.

TRIP TIP

Poison ivy can cause a painful, itchy rash. Learn what it looks like so you can avoid it. The saying, leaves of three, let them be, will help you to identify it.

KEEPING TRAILS CLEAN

The best hikers leave trails the same or better than they found them. Be a respectful hiker. Follow the park or trail rules about bringing pets and making campfires. Carry out your trash and pick up any you find so you can dispose of it properly. Explore and touch, never destroy or collect. Take pictures and write a journal to share and remember your adventure.

Take pictures of landmarks and then point them out on a map to develop map-reading skills.

Protect fragile plants and avoid getting lost by staying on the trail.

PLEASE STAY ON TRAIL

TRIP TIP
Writing down your experiences remains one of the best ways to remember what made your hike special. You might note the weather, animals you saw, and the names of the trails you followed.

Hiking leads to new friends, good health, and appreciation for the natural world. Spending time outdoors encourages understanding and respect. Our Earth needs young people who care about it and who will protect it. Strap on a pack and hit the trails!

GLOSSARY

compass (KUHM-puhss): a handheld tool that uses a magnetic pointer to show the direction north

geocaching (JEE-oh-cash-ing): an outdoor sport in which players find hidden objects using clues, maps, and a wayfinder, like a compass or GPS

GPS (JEE PEE ESS): stands for Global Positioning System, a handheld electronic device that uses satellite signals from space to pinpoint location

public lands (PUHB-lick LANDZ): lands open for use by all people and often managed by a government agency

synthetics (sihn-THEH-tihks): fabrics, like nylon and polyester, made from plastics and other man-made materials

ticks (TICKS): very small, dark, flat creatures, that attach themselves to people and animals and drink their blood

traction (TRACK-shuhn): grip that keeps a person or thing from slipping

trailhead (TRAYL-hehd): the place where hikers enter and leave a trail system

INDEX

WEBSITES TO VISIT

www.rei.com

americanhiking.org

trails.com

SHOW WHAT YOU KNOW

1. Why is it important to never go hiking alone?

2. What is geocaching?

3. Why should you tuck your pants into your socks when hiking?

4. Name a famous trail in North America.

5. What items should you keep in your first aid kit?